NATIONAL
GEOGRAPHIC

D0602851

Make a Piñata!

Michelle Freeman

We are going to make a piñata.
We need all of these things.

paints

newspapers

string

brushes

candy

bowl

water

spoon

flour

tape

balloons

crepe paper

glitter

3

First, we blow up a balloon.

Next, we mix flour and water to
make a paste.

Then, we tear newspaper into strips.

We dip each newspaper strip in the paste.

Next, we cover the balloon with the wet newspaper strips.

We wrap two long pieces of string
around the balloon so we can hang it.

Then, we cover the balloon with more wet newspaper strips.

We let the newspaper strips
dry overnight.

In the morning, we pop the balloon and pull it out of the piñata.

Then, we fill the piñata with candy and close the opening with tape.

Next, we paint the piñata to look like a fish.

We add crepe paper fins and
put glitter on the scales.

Who can break the piñata?